CELEB ★★ TV STAR

CLARE HIBBERT

W

FRANKLIN WATTS
LONDON • SYDNEY

First published in 2010 by
Franklin Watts
338 Euston Road
London NW1 3BH

Franklin Watts Australia
Level 17/207 Kent Street
Sydney NSW 2000

ISBN: 978 0 7496 9266 7

Dewey classification number: 791.4'5'092

A CIP catalogue record for this book is available from the British Library.

Planning and production by Discovery Books Limited
Managing editor: Laura Durman
Editor: Clare Hibbert
Designer: D.R. Ink
Picture research: Tom Humphrey
Thanks to Saba Douglas-Hamilton, Lauren Ferguson, Danielle Huson, Jo Sarsby Personal
Management Ltd and Sonali Shah

Printed in China

Franklin Watts is a division of Hachette Children's Books, an Hachette UK company.
www.hachette.co.uk

Photo acknowledgements: Des Willie Photography: p 16; Getty Images: cover (Jon Furniss/
Wirelmage), pp 6 (Daniel Berehulak), 7 (Kevin Winter), 8 (Samir Hussein), 9 (Peter
Macdiarmid), 10 (Dan Kitwood), 21 (Dave Hogan), 22 (Simon Bruty/Staff), 23 (Dave Hogan),
24 (Gareth Davies), 24–25 (Claire Greenway); Rowan Musgrave: pp 18–19; Rex Features: pp
1 and 20 (ITV), 4–5 (Ken McKay), 11, 14–15 (Julian Makey), 26 (David Fisher), 27, 28 (Sipa
Press), 29 (Jeff Vespa/Wirelmage); Sonali Shah: pp 12 and 31; Shutterstock Images: p 3
(Edvard Molnar).

CONTENTS

Celebrity Presenters	ANT & DEC	4
TV Talent	SIMON COWELL	6
Fast Shows	RICHARD HAMMOND	8
Comedians	HARRY HILL	10
News Hounds	SONALI SHAH	12
Celebrity Chefs	JAMIE OLIVER	14
Gadgets & Gizmos	ORTIS DELEY	16
Wildlife	SABA DOUGLAS-HAMILTON	18
Game Show Hosts	VERNON KAY	20
Sports Presenters	GARY LINEKER	22
Chatterbox	MIQUITA OLIVER	24
Teen Drama	HOLLYOAKS	26
Real-Life Adventures	PARIS HILTON	28
Glossary		30
Further Information		31
Index		32

ANT & DEC

FACT

Ant & Dec had a short-lived pop career as 'PJ & Duncan' – the names of the characters they played on *Byker Grove*!

Ant (left) & Dec presenting *Britain's Got Talent* on ITV.

It's hard to imagine life without TV! And it's hard to imagine television without celebrities. These personalities come into our very own living rooms to entertain us. No wonder we sometimes feel as if we know them!

Star quality

It takes true talent to become a TV personality, and plenty of determination. Some stars, like double act Ant & Dec, are all-round entertainers. Others are especially good at one thing, such as interviewing other celebrities. Whether they present quiz shows or factual programmes, TV celebs have to hold our attention – or we'll switch over!

Ant & Dec presenting *SM:tv* with Cat Deeley.

Making it

Ant & Dec (Anthony McPartlin and Declan Donnelly) met in 1990 as teen actors on *Byker Grove*, a children's drama series. Dec had seen an advert in a local newspaper calling for cast members. Ant already had TV experience, presenting a kids' activity programme called *Why Don't You?* After *Byker Grove*, the pair teamed up to host children's TV shows, including *Gimme 5*, *The Ant & Dec Show* and *SM:tv* (with Cat Deeley).

Big audiences

The duo's cheeky brand of humour made them a popular choice for prime-time TV. With their twinkly eyes and quick-fire banter, Ant & Dec have been the perfect hosts for big shows such as *Saturday Night Takeaway*, *Britain's Got Talent* and *I'm a Celebrity... Get Me out of Here!* They've also presented *Soccer Aid* and other charity extravaganzas.

CELEB BIO

Dates of birth **Ant 18 November 1975, Dec 25 September 1975**

Places of birth **Newcastle-upon-Tyne (Ant), Draperstown, Northern Ireland (Dec)**

Key shows ***The Ant & Dec Show, Ant & Dec Unzipped, Saturday Night Takeaway, Britain's Got Talent***

Greatest achievement **Winning Most Popular Entertainment Presenter at the National Television Awards seven years in a row**

'You're somebody and nobody in a split second. This is a business. You can only look out for yourself... or in our case each other.' ANT

SIMON COWELL

Televised talent shows took off at the end of the 1990s. These reality programmes allow ordinary members of the public to show off their singing or performing skills and become stars. The judges on these programmes find fame and wealth, too!

Reality TV

Popstars, *Pop Idol* and *The X Factor* are all reality TV shows that seek out musical talent. Simon Cowell appeared as a judge on *Pop Idol* when it launched in 2001. The programme's success inspired him to create his own version, *The X Factor*, in 2007. Although *Pop Idol* is no longer broadcast in the UK, *American Idol* goes from strength to strength. Cowell is a judge on that, too!

Early career

Cowell started out in the music business, working his way up from postroom boy to A&R executive. The artists he discovered and promoted in the 1980s and 1990s included Sinitta, Sonia, Robson & Jerome, Five and Westlife. After years behind the scenes, Cowell's TV career placed him in the spotlight. His knowledge of pop made him the perfect judge of the contestants' talent.

Character assassin

Cowell is such an onscreen success because he can be nasty and funny at the same time. Cowell's catchphrase is 'I don't mean to be rude but…' – which he says just before he's jaw-droppingly rude about a contestant. He's the judge that viewers love to hate.

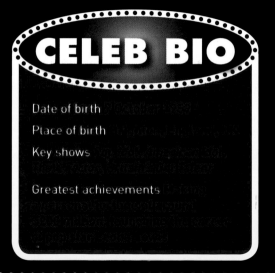

CELEB BIO

Date of birth

Place of birth

Key shows

Greatest achievements

'I don't mean
to be rude, but
you look like
the Incredible
Hulk's wife.'

Cowell on the set of
American Idol.

'I was brought up to be adventurous and ambitious and to try to think about other people.'

RICHARD HAMMOND

Shows about vehicles, motoring and fast cars are extremely popular, especially with male viewers. There's even a whole cable channel devoted to these kinds of programmes in the UK, called Men & Motors.

Starting out

Men & Motors gave Richard Hammond his first break on television, as a presenter of various lifestyle and motoring programmes. He had begun his career in radio, working his way up from hospital radio to local stations.

Top Gear

Hammond moved over to mainstream TV in 2002. *Top Gear*, a 25-year-old motoring show on BBC2, was just being relaunched. Instead of having a single presenter, it was going to have three: Jeremy Clarkson, Hammond and James May. The trio showcase new cars and other vehicles. They also tease each other and compete in silly races.

Crash survivor

In 2006 Hammond suffered a near-fatal crash while test-driving a high-speed jet car for *Top Gear*. Amazingly, he survived and recovered – despite terrible brain injuries. The crash was broadcast on the show when Hammond was fit to return in January 2007.

Celebrity science and crazy games

Before the crash, Hammond had hosted the first four series of *Brainiac: Science Abuse*, a funny, popular science show on Sky. He stuck with the theme for *Blast Lab*, in which two teams of children compete to solve science-based problems. He also presents *Total Wipeout*, a show with adult contestants who compete on a series of assault courses while Hammond provides an amusing commentary.

The *Top Gear* team – Clarkson (left), May (centre) and Hammond (right) – take a ride on a tank.

Featuring

MPH
THE PRESTIGE & PERFORMANCE MOTOR SHOW

TopGear Live

MPH
THE PRESTIGE & PERFORMANCE MOTOR SHOW

Featuring TopGear Live

CELEB BIO

Date of birth **19 December 1969**

Place of birth **Solihull, West Midlands, UK**

Key shows **Top Gear, *Richard Hammond's Blast Lab*, *Total Wipeout***

Greatest achievements **Winning the Royal Society's Junior Prize for Science Books twice; winning a TRIC (Television and Radio Industries Club) Best Satellite/ Digital TV Personality Award**

HARRY HILL

TV comedians are the modern equivalent of court jesters! Comedy shows take a variety of formats. Some are recordings of live stand-up acts with lots of jokes and banter. Others are sketch shows – collections of short comic scenes.

FACT

In 2006 Harry Hill published his first children's story. *Tim the Tiny Horse* is about a horse so tiny that it lives in a matchbox.

One-of-a-kind

Harry Hill has created his own unique and madcap kind of comedy. He trained as a doctor, but stand-up was his true calling. After he won an award for Best Newcomer at the Edinburgh Fringe Festival in 1992, the BBC commissioned *Harry Hill's Fruit Corner* for Radio 4. The show became a TV series in 1994.

TV success

In 1997 Channel 4 launched *The Harry Hill Show*. The programme featured a whole host of regular characters, jokes and songs. Every show, Hill promised a parade of cuddly-toy badgers – but something always stopped the parade from happening.

Dressing the part

Like many TV stars, Harry Hill has a trademark look. He's known for his bald head, black-rimmed glasses, outsize collars, wide-lapelled suits and thick-soled shoes known as 'brothel creepers'. He also has catchphrases, such as 'You've got to have a system' and 'What are the chances of that happening?'.

Other shows

Harry Hill has hosted other programmes. *Harry Hill's TV Burp* on ITV looks at clips from the week's television. Hill points out funny links between shows and draws attention to silly dialogue or facial expressions. *Harry Hill's Shark-Infested Custard* aired on CITV in 2005. Hill has also guest-starred on other children's shows, including *Chucklevision* and *Blue Peter*.

Hill promoting The Wonderbus Project, a charity that provides days out for the elderly.

CELEB BIO

Real name **Matthew Hall**

Date of birth **1 October 1964**

Place of birth **Woking, Surrey, UK**

Key shows *The Harry Hill Show, Harry Hill's TV Burp*

Greatest achievement **Winning three BAFTAs for *Harry Hill's TV Burp***

'Mangetouts, they're lovely aren't they? But I couldn't eat a whole one.'

'What makes a good *Newsround* story? Anything that keeps you watching!'

News and current affairs programmes are among the most important on TV. Although we can also find out what's happening in the world from radio, newspapers and other media, many of us rely on television news.

SONALI SHAH

Reporting and presenting

Some TV news presenters begin their careers as reporters for local TV stations. Others, like *Newsround* presenter Sonali Shah, start out in radio instead. Shah read business news for the BBC World Service and, later, Radio 5 Live. In 2006 she heard that *Newsround* was looking for a new presenter.

Getting the job

Shah sent the *Newsround* producers a tape showing off her previous work, and was asked to do a screen test. Her friendly face and clear speaking voice won her the job! At first, she read the morning bulletins. In 2008 she became co-chief anchor of the afternoon show (sharing the job with Ore Oduba).

Reading the news

Reading the news demands special skills. Shah reads the words of the story as they scroll down a computer screen (an autocue). She says the words as naturally as she can. It's OK for her to smile or even giggle – so long as the story's a funny one.

Special interests

Newsround is aimed at young viewers, so it covers stories that really matter to them. In 2008 Shah went to Beijing, China, to report on the Olympics for *Newsround* and its sister programme, *Sportsround*. Shah has also presented *Newsround Specials*, including one about knife crime.

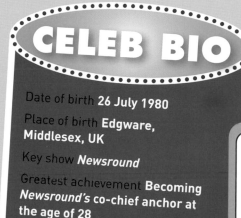

CELEB BIO

Date of birth **26 July 1980**

Place of birth **Edgware, Middlesex, UK**

Key show *Newsround*

Greatest achievement Becoming *Newsround's* co-chief anchor at the age of 28

FACT

Newsround was originally named *John Craven's Newsround*, after its creator. Craven presented the show for 17 years, from 1972 to 1989.

The *Newsround* team on their website. From left to right: Ore Oduba, Leah Gooding, Sonali Shah, Hayley Cutts and Ricky Boleto.

CELEBRITY CHEFS

Television is a great place to inform viewers how to do things. TV chefs host programmes that show people how to cook. They publish recipe books to accompany their series, but it's their TV appearances that make them stars.

Early years

Celebrity chefs are not new. Fanny Cradock was a famous cook in the 1950s. Her programmes were in black and white, with Cradock wearing a chiffon gown and spotless apron. She cooked complicated, French-influenced dishes. Food became even more elaborate in the 1970s when the American Robert Carrier came to our screens.

A new generation

The 1990s saw changes in food fashion. People wanted fresh ingredients cooked simply so the flavours shone through. Jamie Oliver reflected this trend. He was the first really young TV chef, making his debut aged just 23. Not bad for someone with dyslexia, who left school with no qualifications!

'Pukka!'

After catering college Oliver had worked in two of London's leading Italian restaurants, Neal's Yard and the River Café. A BBC producer spotted him and commissioned the *Naked Chef* series. Oliver's chirpy, relaxed approach was an instant hit. Audiences loved him throwing in a splash of this and a handful of that.

Important issues

Oliver began to use his celebrity to educate people about food. In *Jamie's Kitchen* he trained young people from difficult backgrounds to work in his restaurant, Fifteen. *Jamie's School Dinners* helped improve nutrition in schools. *Jamie's Ministry of Food* taught ordinary people to cook instead of buying ready meals.

CELEB BIO

Date of birth 27 May 1975

Place of birth Clavering, Essex, UK

Key shows *The Naked Chef, Jamie's Kitchen, Jamie's School Dinners*

Greatest achievements Being awarded an MBE in 2003, cooking for world leaders at the G20 summit

JAMIE OLIVER

Oliver promoting his show, *Jamie's School Dinners*.

'All I ever wanted to do was to make food accessible to everyone; to show that you can make mistakes – I do all the time – but it doesn't matter.'

FACT

The BBC's flagship gadget show *Tomorrow's World* ran for 38 years! In 2001 Ortis Deley presented a *Tomorrow's World* spin-off called *Lab Rats*.

Ortis Deley on the set of *The Gadget Show*.

'The human ability to create ever more impressive technology never fails to astound me.'

ORTIS DELEY

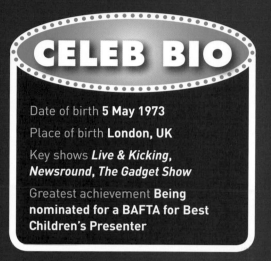

CELEB BIO

Date of birth **5 May 1973**

Place of birth **London, UK**

Key shows *Live & Kicking, Newsround, The Gadget Show*

Greatest achievement **Being nominated for a BAFTA for Best Children's Presenter**

Consumer shows allow television viewers to find out about all the latest products. Some of these look at gadgets and technology. It's exciting seeing must-have gizmos being put through their paces!

Techno TV

The TV channel Five first broadcast *The Gadget Show* in 2004. Since the seventh series, the show's been extended from 45 minutes to an hour. There's a lot to pack in! The format is to look at new gadgets and review their performance. There are also news items about breaking technology – everything from cars to robots.

Deley on TV

The Gadget Show has four presenters: Suzi Perry, Jon Bentley, Jason Bradbury and Ortis Deley. Ortis Deley joined in 2009. His first TV appearance was 14 years earlier, as a contestant on the dating game show, *Blind Date*. He had such charisma that programme makers at LWT (London Weekend Television) asked him to present a new breakfast show.

Trouble and the Beeb

Deley went on to establish his career presenting youth programmes on the cable channel, Trouble. *It's in the Jeans* looked at boy-girl relationships, while *Blast* and *iPop* focused on the charts. Next, Deley moved to the BBC to present a children's consumer affairs programme, *Short Change*. Other projects included *Xchange* (a magazine programme of celebrities, music and fun), *Best of Friends* (a game show) and science-based programmes such as *Why 5* and *X-perimental*.

Ortis the actor

Deley's also taken on acting roles. He has appeared in films, such as *Kidulthood*, as well as several TV series, including *Doctors* and *The Bill*.

SABA DOUGLAS-HAMILTON

'The reason I make films is to inspire people about the beauty of the natural world... I believe passionately that if you love something then you will want to protect it.'

Few of us can go in person to see turtles lay eggs, snow leopards hunt, whales dive, or experience being charged by an elephant. Wildlife programmes give us a front-row seat to observe all sorts of weird and wonderful animal behaviour.

Experts

Nature programmes are usually presented by scientists who have studied animal biology and behaviour at university and out in the field. One pioneer of this kind of TV is David Attenborough, who has spent more than 50 years making natural history programmes for the BBC. Saba Douglas-Hamilton, the daughter of elephant conservationists in Kenya, is part of a new generation of inspiring wildlife presenters.

Monkeying around

Douglas-Hamilton's first job for the BBC was *Going Ape*, broadcast in 2002. Rather bravely, she lived with a troop of chimps in the rainforest of West Africa with nothing but the clothes on her back. She ate termites and wild fruit, slept in a hammock – and relied on the troop to wake her if a leopard came near.

Out of Africa

Since then, Douglas-Hamilton has made many programmes in her native Africa, documenting the lives of rhinos, elephants, leopards, lions, gorillas and camels. She's also filmed in different climates, including the icy poles, where she studied polar bears and penguins.

Animal values

Wild animals can be unpredictable, but Douglas-Hamilton relishes the challenge and thinks the danger's worth it. As a committed conservationist, she knows the importance of educating people about animals, especially endangered ones – before it's too late.

FACT

Douglas-Hamilton had interesting pets as a child, including a pet mongoose and a warthog!

CELEB BIO

Date of birth **7 June 1970**

Place of birth **Kenya, Africa**

Key shows ***Big Cat Diary/Week, Running with Reindeer, Search for Tigers, Secret Life of Elephants***

Greatest achievements **Filming a secret gathering of black rhino in the desert; becoming a Trustee for Save the Elephants**

VERNON KAY

Whether the competitors are celebrities or ordinary members of the public, game shows can be great to watch. Their success depends on how interesting and challenging the game is – and how entertaining the host is!

Special skills

Game show hosts don't necessarily tell jokes, but their shows need to make people smile. A gentle jibe at the competitors' expense raises a laugh, but no one wants to see them feeling uncomfortable. It's a fine balance.

Prime time

With his friendly face and boy-next-door appeal, Vernon Kay's a natural. He was chosen to host *Family Fortunes* when it relaunched in 2006 (previously, it ran from 1980 until 2002). Kay had a lot to live up to, since previous presenters had included light-entertainment legend Bob Monkhouse.

Route to the top

Kay came to TV via modelling. He was spotted by a modelling agency scout at the BBC's *Clothes Show Live*. The agency put him into a modelling contest on Channel 4's *The Big Breakfast* – and he won! He was so good on that show that programme makers asked him to host *T in the Park* soon after.

Talents and technique

Kay has the knack of putting just about anyone at ease. This talent has stood him in good stead on *Family Fortunes* and on *Beat the Star*, a game show where a contestant takes on a celebrity in various games and challenges.

CELEB BIO

Date of birth **28 April 1974**

Place of birth **Bolton, Lancashire, UK**

Key shows **HeadJam, Boys and Girls, Celebrities Under Pressure, Family Fortunes**

Greatest achievements **Interviewing the elusive Richard Ashcroft for T4; relaunching Family Fortunes**

Kay on the set of *Beat the Star*.

'I've always wanted to work on TV. It's a bit of a cliché but I was always the kid at school making a fool of himself.'

GARY LINEKER

On air since 1964, *Match of the Day* is one of the BBC's longest-running shows. It used to be the only TV programme where football fans could get the lowdown on the day's fixtures. These days, there's plenty of competition from cable and satellite channels, but the show remains popular.

From pundit to presenter

Match of the Day has a history of choosing expert presenters – world-class players and coaches who know the 'beautiful game' inside out. Gary Lineker joined the show as a pundit in 1995, and took over as the anchor in 1999, when Des Lynam left.

Pitch career

Between the ages of 18 and 34, Lineker had a long and successful career as a striker, starting out at Leicester City and playing for Everton and Spurs, as well as overseas clubs Barcelona (Spain) and Nagoya Grampus Eight (Japan).

Move to media

After retiring from football, Lineker moved into the media. He appeared on *Match of the Day*, as well as the sports game show, *They Think It's All Over*. He has also provided the voice for the commentary of several PlayStation football games – and for the CBeebies character, Underground Ernie. He played himself in the feature film *Bend It Like Beckham*.

Comic crisp ads

In 1995, Lineker began appearing in adverts for Walkers Crisps. The ads play with his reputation as a trustworthy 'nice guy' by casting him as a villainous crisp-stealer!

Lineker celebrates after scoring for England against West Germany in the 1990 World Cup semi-final.

'I've been incredibly fortunate to have found a couple of things I can do: football and television.'

Lineker poses with his TRIC Best Sports Presenter Award in 2009.

CELEB BIO

Date of birth **30 November 1960**

Place of birth **Leicester, UK**

Football clubs **Leicester City, Everton, FC Barcelona, Tottenham Hotspur, Nagoya Grampus Eight**

Key TV appearances *Match of the Day*, adverts for Walkers Crisps

Greatest achievement **Winning the Golden Boot (being top goal scorer) in the 1986 World Cup**

'I interviewed Justin Timberlake when I was 18 and I was so nervous I couldn't breathe properly.'

MIQUITA OLIVER

Miquita and *Popworld* co-presenter Simon Amstell with singer Estelle.

Youth TV demands particular talents of its presenters – most of all a cheeky, bubbly personality. Add to that good looks, a strong fashion sense and the ability to think on your feet – and you have the perfect pop-culture anchor.

Famous family

Miquita Oliver comes from a celebrity family. Her aunt is the singer Neneh Cherry and her mother was in the post-punk band Rip Rig + Panic. Oliver was still doing her GCSEs when she began co-presenting C4's irreverent music show, *Popworld*, with comedian Simon Amstell. At the audition, she had to demonstrate her knowledge of pop by naming all the members of the boy band Five.

Youth TV

Oliver went on to make her name presenting for *T4* – Channel 4's teen TV programme – co-hosting and interviewing pop acts in the studio and at live shows around the country. In the course of her career, she has chatted to such big names as Justin Timberlake, Beyoncé, Lady GaGa, The Saturdays and McFly. Of course she sometimes get star struck – but she never gets tongue-tied!

Music…

Oliver's sassy onscreen persona also provided the perfect vehicle for a series of shows called *Miquita Does…*, which explored particular musical styles or phenomena, such as power ballads or number-one hits.

… and more!

It won't be long before Oliver becomes a regular pundit on more serious shows, acting as an expert on popular culture. She has already guested on BBC1's news review programme *This Week*, discussing the significance of politicians' fashions!

Many TV celebrities make their name on 'soaps'. These are ongoing dramas with intense, gripping storylines that usually air several times a week, with a weekly omnibus for catching up on those essential missed episodes.

HOLLYOAKS

Big audiences

Coronation Street (more than 13 million viewers) and *Eastenders* (nearly 12 million viewers) are the two biggest UK soaps – but for younger audiences, the must-see show is *Hollyoaks*.

Student setting

Hollyoaks launched on Channel 4 in 1995. It was the creation of Phil Redmond, who had come up with the idea of the Liverpool-based soap, *Brookside*, about a decade earlier. The show is set in a fictional Chester suburb, called Hollyoaks, and focuses on students at the local college. Central characters include Newt (Barry Newton), played by Nico Mirallegro, and Anita Roy, played by Saira Choudhry. Both Mirallegro and Choudhry studied drama at the Manchester School of Acting. The school put them forward for *Hollyoaks* auditions.

Big issues

Like all soaps, *Hollyoaks'* plot revolves around relationships – between family members, couples and friends. At the same time, its storylines address bigger issues, including homelessness, drug addiction, shoplifting and teenage pregnancy. Different characters take centre-stage at different times.

Challenging roles

The roles are challenging for the young actors. Being Newt doesn't just involve wearing a wig and eyeliner! Mirallegro has had to learn all about schizophrenia. For the character of Anita, Choudhry has had to research adoption and racial bullying.

Nico Mirallegro attending the British Soap Awards.

'It's been great to play Newt, great from an actor's point of view to play such a challenging role and also to highlight such an important issue [mental illness]...' NICO

Saira Choudhry (left) with fellow *Hollyoaks* star Dominique Jackson who plays Lauren Valentine.

CELEB BIO

Years of birth **Nico Mirallegro 1988, Saira Choudhry 1991**

Place of birth **Manchester, UK**

Key shows *Hollyoaks, LOL* (Nico)

Greatest achievements **Winning their *Hollyoaks* roles; two British Soap Award nominations (Nico)**

Paris Hilton (left) and Nicole Richie (right) work on a dairy farm for *The Simple Life*.

PARIS HILTON

'The only rule is don't be boring and dress cute wherever you go. Life is too short to blend in.'

Reality TV has made ordinary members of the public famous because of how they've coped onscreen with strange, new experiences. However, reality shows can be even more gripping when their stars are already celebs.

Poor little rich girls

The American heiress and socialite Paris Hilton found TV fame with *The Simple Life*, on which she co-starred with her real-life friend, Nicole Richie. The idea of the show was very simple – to take two spoiled rich girls and to place them each week in a different unskilled, low-paid job.

Winning formula

The Simple Life proved to be television gold! There was comedy in the girls' ridiculous, inappropriate clothing – and their failure to rise to challenges such as milking cows or making sausages. And then there was the gossipy drama of the girls' onscreen bickering.

Friendly follow-ons

Hilton and Richie's public falling-out ended their collaboration on *The Simple Life* but also helped to inspire Hilton's next show. *Paris Hilton's My New BFF*, about her search for a new 'best friend forever'. There have also been spin-offs, including her hunt for a British best friend.

Hilton's life

Hilton started her career as a model. Then she had several small parts in movies before landing *The Simple Life*. A brief spell in jail in 2007 – she violated her probation terms after a conviction for reckless driving – has not really harmed her career. If anything, she has benefited from the publicity.

CELEB BIO

Date of birth **17 February 1981**

Place of birth **New York City, USA**

Key shows ***The Simple Life, Paris Hilton's My New BFF, Paris Hilton's British Best Friend***

Greatest achievements **Founding her own record label; launching fragrances and her own fashion ranges**

FACT

Paris's great grandfather founded the Hilton chain of hotels.

GLOSSARY

A&R executive Short for 'Artists and Repertoire'. An A&R executive's job is to find new talent and then to support artists, helping them to record their music and keep a good relationship with the record label.

anchor The main presenter of a programme, especially a news programme.

audition A short performance given by a presenter or actor to show that he or she would be suitable for a particular show or role.

banter Friendly, playful conversation.

catchphrase A well-known saying or phrase, especially one that is associated with a particular person.

clip A short extract from a television programme or film.

commission To ask someone to create something. For example, a programme maker may commission a television star to write or present a new programme.

conservationist Someone who works hard to save or restore wildlife and habitats.

current affairs All the important things that are happening in the world right now.

documentary A factual television programme or film.

dyslexia A learning difficulty that affects language skills, such as reading ability.

endangered Describes an animal or plant that is in danger of becoming extinct (dying out forever).

format The particular way in which a programme is organized.

light entertainment Programmes on television that do not try to teach or challenge, but simply to amuse and entertain, for example game shows and variety shows, involving music, magic and light comedy.

natural history A science that looks at the lives of animals and plants.

omnibus A long edition of a show, especially a soap opera, that comprises all of the episodes aired in the last week.

presenter Someone who introduces and appears in a television programme.

prime time The time of day or week that attracts the largest television audiences.

pundit An expert who appears on television or in other media to express an opinion on something.

reality TV An unscripted TV show starring people (being themselves, not acting) facing challenging events, such as living together in a house, taking part in a talent contest or trying out a new job.

schizophrenia A severe mental disorder, characterised by 'split personality' – the disturbing feeling that you are not one person but a collection of different people.

scout Someone employed by an organization, for example a modelling agency, to find new talent.

soap opera An ongoing drama series on television or radio that contains a large cast of characters with interconnected lives.

socialite A prominent member of high society, often going to lots of parties.

spin-off Something that owes its existence to something else that came first. Spin-off television programmes take ideas, formats or characters from existing shows and use them to create new shows.

stand-up Describes a particular kind of comic performance, in which a comedian stands on stage before the live audience, delivering jokes.

storyline The main theme or plot of a drama.

talent contest A competition that rewards the most gifted contestant.

BOOKS

21st Century Lives: Celebrity Chefs by Debbie Foy (Wayland, 2010)

21st Century Lives: Reality TV Stars by Adam Sutherland (Wayland, 2009)

21st Century Lives: Soap Stars by Debbie Foy (Wayland, 2009)

21st Century Lives: TV Celebrities by Liz Gogerly (Wayland, 2007)

Harry Hill's TV Burp Book by Harry Hill (Ebury, 2009)

Livewire Real Lives: Ant & Dec by Andy Croft (Hodder Murray, 2005)

Modern Role Models: American Idol Panel by Jim Whiting (Mason Crest, 2009)

Newsround Year Book (BBC Children's books, published annually)

Pop Culture: Paris and Nicky Hilton by Emma Carlson Berne (Mason Crest, 2007)

Richard Hammond's Blast Lab by Richard Hammond (Dorling Kindersley, 2009)

DVDS

Big Cat Week: The Complete Fourth Series (2 Entertain Video, 2008)

Gary Lineker's Action Replay (Liberation Entertainment, 2007)

Jamie at Home (Fremantle Home Entertainment, 2007)

Richard Hammond's Top Gear *Uncovered* (2 Entertain Video, 2009)

Top Gear Collection (2 Entertain Video, 2006)

WEBSITES

www.bbc.co.uk/tv
The area of the BBC website that provides information on BBC programmes and presenters.

www.itv.com
The official website of ITV, with information on programmes such as *The X Factor* and *Britain's Got Talent*.

www.channel4.com/entertainment/t4
The area of the Channel 4 website that provides information on *T4* programmes, including *T4 at the Beach*, *Hollyoaks* and *Frock Me*.

adverts 22
American Idol 6, 7
Amstell, Simon 25
Ant & Dec 4–5
Ant & Dec Show, The 5
Attenborough, David 19
autocues 13
awards
    BAFTAs 10, 17
    British Soap Awards 26, 27
    Edinburgh Comedy Awards 10
    MBEs 14
    National Television Awards 5
    TRIC Awards 9, 23

Beat the Star 20
Bend It Like Beckham 22
Best of Friends 17
Beyoncé 25
Big Breakfast, The 20
Big Cat Diary 19
Bill, The 17
Blast 17
Blast Lab 8, 9
Brainiac: Science Abuse 8
Britain's Got Talent 4, 5, 6
Brookside 26
Byker Grove 4, 5

Carrier, Robert 14
charities 5, 10
children's programmes 5, 8, 10, 17, 22
Choudhry, Saira 26, 27
Clarkson, Jeremy 8, 9
comedy 10–11
consumer programmes 16–17
cookery programmes 14–15
Coronation Street 26
Cowell, Simon 6–7
Cradock, Fanny 14
current affairs 12–13, 25

Deeley, Cat 5
Deley, Ortis 16–17
Doctors 17
Douglas-Hamilton, Saba 18–19
dyslexia 14

Eastenders 26

Family Fortunes 20, 21
Five (boy band) 6, 25

Gadget Show, The 16, 17
game shows 8, 17, 20–21, 22
Gimme 5 5
Going Ape 19

Hammond, Richard 8–9
Harry Hill Show, The 10
Harry Hill's TV Burp 10
Hill, Harry 10–11
Hilton, Paris 28–29
Hollyoaks 26–27

I'm a Celebrity… Get Me out of Here! 5
iPop 17
It's in the Jeans 17

Jackson, Dominique 27
Jamie's Kitchen 14
Jamie's Ministry of Food 14
Jamie's School Dinners 14–15

Kay, Vernon 20–21
Kidulthood 17

Lady GaGa 25
Lineker, Gary 22–23
Live & Kicking 17
Lynam, Des 22

Match of the Day 22
May, James 8
McFly 25
Men & Motors 8
Miquita Does… 25
Mirallegro, Nico 26, 27
modelling 20
Monkhouse, Bob 20

Naked Chef, The 14, 15
news programmes 12–13, 25
Newsround 12, 13, 17

Oduba, Ore 13
Oliver, Jamie 14–15
Oliver, Miquita 24–25

Paris Hilton's British Best Friend 29
Paris Hilton's My New BFF 29
PJ & Duncan *see* Ant & Dec
Pop Idol 6
pop stars 4, 6, 24, 25
Popstars 6
Popworld 25

radio 8, 13
reality TV 6–7, 28–29
Redmond, Phil 26
Richie, Nicole 28, 29

Saturday Night Takeaway 5
Saturdays, The 25
science programmes 8, 17
screen tests 13
Shah, Sonali 12–13
Short Change 17
Simple Life, The 28, 29
Simpsons, The 6
SM:tv 5
soaps 26–27
Soccer Aid 5
sports programmes 13, 22–23

T in the Park 20
T4 20, 25
talent shows 4, 5, 6–7
They Think It's All Over 22
Timberlake, Justin 25
Tomorrow's World 16, 17
Top Gear 8, 9
Total Wipeout 8, 9

Why 5 17
Why Don't You? 5
wildlife programmes 18–19

X Factor, The 6
X-perimental 17
Xchange 17

youth programmes 17, 24–25, 26–27